Lives of the Animals

POEMS BY

Robert Wrigley

Lives of the Animals

PENGUIN POETS

PENGUIN BOOKS
Published by the Penguin Group
Penguin Group (USA) Inc., 375 Hudson Street,
New York, New York 10014, U.S.A.
Penguin Books Ltd, 80 Strand, London WC2R 0RL, England
Penguin Books Australia Ltd, 250 Camberwell Road, Camberwell, Victoria 3124, Australia
Penguin Books Canada Ltd, 10 Alcorn Avenue,
Toronto, Ontario, Canada M4V 3B2
Penguin Books India (P) Ltd, 11 Community Centre,
Panchsheel Park, New Delhi - 110 017, India
Penguin Books (N.Z.) Ltd, Cnr Rosedale and Airborne Roads, Albany,
Auckland, New Zealand
Penguin Books (South Africa) (Pty) Ltd, 24 Sturdee Avenue,
Rosebank, Johannesburg 2196, South Africa

Penguin Books Ltd, Registered Offices:
80 Strand, London WC2R 0RL, England

First published in Penguin Books 2003

3 5 7 9 10 8 6 4

Copyright © Robert Wrigley, 2003
All rights reserved

Page ix constitutes an extension of this copyright page.

LIBRARY OF CONGRESS CATALOGING IN PUBLICATION DATA
Wrigley, Robert, date.
Lives of the animals / Robert Wrigley.
p. cm.
ISBN 0-14-200345-X
I. Title.
PS3573.R58L59 2003
811'.54—dc21   2003045618

Printed in the United States of America
Set in Throhand
Designed by Ginger Legato

FOR KIM

ACKNOWLEDGMENTS

The author would like to express his gratitude to the editors of the following periodicals, in which many of these poems first appeared.

The Alaska Quarterly Review: Anecdotal Fencepost

The Atlantic Monthly: Discretion; Highway 12, Just East of Paradise, Idaho; The Other World; Winter Bale

Barrow Street: Thatcher Bitchboy

Beloit Poetry Journal: After the Coyotes' Song

Connections: Bridge

Crab Orchard Review: Snake in the Trough

Five Points: Washing My Face

The Georgia Review: Later That Day; Myopia; Sweetbreads

The Gettysburg Review: Explanatory; Following Snakes

Gulf Coast: Caffeine; Northern Lights; Poor Animals

The Kenyon Review: Agency; Clemency; Mummy of a Mouse

Manoa: The Church of Omnivorous Light; In an Abandoned Orchard; Lives of the Animals

Margie: Mercy

Permafrost: Elk Dreams

Poetry: At the Beach; Do You Love Me?; Fish Dreams; Progress; Swallows

Rattapallax: Kissing a Horse

Shenandoah: Breaking Trail

Slate (http://slate.msn.com): Quiet Night

Sou'wester: Affirmations; Helpful

The Southern Review: The Afterlife of Moose; In Time

The Virginia Quarterly Review: Bear Dreams; "Dog"

The Church of Omnivorous Light appeared in the *Pushcart Prize XXVII* anthology, 2002.

Several of these poems appeared previously in the chapbook *Clemency*, published in 2002 by Limberlost Press.

Clemency also appeared in *Best American Poetry 2003*. New York: Scribner, 2003.

Highway 12, Just East of Paradise, Idaho appeared in *Poetry 180*, edited by Billy Collins. New York: Random House, 2003.

CONTENTS

And as the dog with its nostrils tracking out the fragments of the beasts' limbs, and the breath from their feet that they leave in the soft grass, runs upon a path that is pathless to men, so does the soul follow the trail of the dead, across great spaces.

—D. H. Lawrence

THE OTHER WORLD

So here is the old buck
    who all winter long
had traveled with the does
    and yearlings, with the fawns
just past their spots,
    and who had hung back,
walking where the others had walked,
    eating what they had left,
and who had struck now and then
    a pose against the wind,
against a limb-snap or the way
    the light came slinking
among the trees.

Here is the mangled ear
    and the twisted, hindering leg.
Here, already bearing him away
    among the last drifts of snow
and the nightly hard freezes,
    is a line of tiny ants,
making its way from the cave
    of the right eye, over the steep
occipital ridge, across the moonscape shed-horn
    medallion and through the valley
of the ear's cloven shadow
    to the ground,
where among the staves
    of shed needles and the red earthy wine
they carry him
    bit by gnawn bit
into another world.

HORSE

After a while you can pick their droppings up —
    horses — and you don't even mind it.
Silver and dun, from a chain of palm-sized
    nestled orbs, hay muffins

and faux stones, the fat pearls
    of peristalsis, night scones
you can crack on a fence wire,
    like eggs quickened and laid by a being

whose truest soul is waiting and running:
    filly with a taste for sugar and salt,
sad-eyed colt with a swayful tail
    and a single, flashy white sock.

ELK DREAMS

for Mark Spragg

1. Rut

For years he could not separate
that old ranch hand's redolence of handrolled smokes
from the whole thing—
braised strap of the elk's back
and its shimmering sent-up pennant, a balm for his lungs,
or the hot redness of rare meat cloven
and laid out before him as a meal—always
the mount and thrust of the bull in that high meadow
and the blunt, blue-nailed, nicotine-tinted index finger
of the old man pointing the way,
and no one saying a word during or after,
and still years later on, when he held a woman
and a branched cloud of dreams swirled from his head
and their risen scents curled upward
and sunlight lay among the bedclothes like ash.

2. Birth

But later he was alone, walking
in spring, and the moistness of the duff
and the silence of dustlessness let him float
inside the wash of the melt-fat creek
and emerge from behind a stone wall
to see smack in the middle of the trail
the elk cow's backside like a meaty rose unfold
and the calf come leapingly squeezed
and sliding to the trail, the cow lurching
forward and the knuckled cord towing forth
the afterbirth, which fell with a wet slap

just as the cow turned, tongue already lolling
for the lick and the quick unloosing of the caul
from the calf, when she saw him there, a boy
who could not move, who could not even breathe,
but who knew exactly what it was he had seen
and how it came to be.

AT THE BEACH

What are they, those burrowing crustaceans,
the ones my son and I unbeach each summer
building sandcastles? Thumb-large
helmets with dainty, iridescent feet
and as far as I can see no eyes,
no head, no front or back at all, only
the shove and pull of the waves,
or only the quick, attentive gulls, who love them
just as they would love us, my son and me, if they could,
and who, the truth be told, cannot name us either.

EXPLANATORY

The hackberry tree, a static of twigs and branches
so densely woven sparrows went flitless there,
but hopped instead, stob to stob, and disappeared
like names, dates, and faces in an ordinary mind.
It was the bowl at the top I wanted to see for myself,
twig-sac of heft and weave, broad
as the hindquarters of a bull, nest of dozen
generations of eagle, heron, or hawk.
I had studied it for an hour and seen no sign of life
but saw a way up, beside the hackberry, up
the thigh-thick limbs of the yellow pine,
then out its long crooked pitch-dripping finger
pointing inside the snarl and bracing maybe
the nest itself. Even then I felt myself the fool I was,
in that deep green chapel climbing,
having lost the brightest light, seeing in every crotch of bark
a voodoo beautiful arrangement of rodents' bones.
I found the limb and sat it well, like a horse,
and skidded my way outward, seeing from under the canopy of needles
how this mount was swallowed in the hackberry's thatch,
how the limbs of one had grown inside the other, until
on the last yard or less I was back in the open, half-blind
and wobbling to my feet, letting my bare, tacky hands ascend
the nest's outer wall. A single foot shy of the lip,
I placed my ear to it, a body of ribs. There was no heart
to be heard beneath the wind blowing by,
though by and by, my eyes at last unblinking, I saw
how just above my cheek a rabbit's skull swayed
in a thong of its own delicate leather, how the last round mound
between my hair and the nest's open maw
was a Joseph's coat of hide and hair. Slowly,
I stalked, lifted my right leg

and nestled it in among the tight-woven branches.
And there was nothing there but my arms, elbows locked
among the stobs and hoisting me up and up, nothing
until the horned owl came out flying,
leaping, hooked beak wide and blue-gray tongue protruding,
a mother-noise a million years old
that even as I fell, screeching myself, I kept on hearing.
It was her talon that tore the palm of my hand,
or a bone or a branch, it was something I held that held
me back, or seemed to as I fell, my legs
by the miracle of it swinging beneath me again,
so that I landed belly-down across the same pitchy branch
I'd entered on, then slung myself sloth-like from it
and dangled there, my eyes twisted shut,
my heart making wing-beat bird after bird,
my breath a mix of man's gasp and rabbit bleat.
And this is why my life and heart lines are joined inside my fist,
a kind of canal of the flesh, a path from knowing to faith.
This is why I have crawled along the thoroughfares of snakes
with a bedsheet, looking to rescue a broken-winged owl.
Therefore, when a grass fire swept toward it, I ran
to that same, swaybacked, fuel-dense hackberry tree
and pummeled it with stones and howled
until they rose—one, two, three, cat-faced and immense—
great horned owls aloft toward the going down sun.

DO YOU LOVE ME?

She's twelve and she's asking the dog,
who does, but who speaks
in tongues, whose feints and gyrations
are themselves parts of speech.

They're on the back porch
and I don't really mean to be taking this in
but once I've heard I can't stop listening. Again
and again she asks, and the good dog

sits and wiggles, leaps and licks.
Imagine never asking. Imagine why:
so sure you wouldn't dare, or couldn't care
less. I wonder if the dog's guileless brown eyes

can lie, if the perfect canine lack of abstractions
might not be a bit like the picture books
she "read" as a child, before her parents' lips
shaped the daily miracle of speech

and kisses, and the words were not lead
and weighed only air, and did not mean
so meanly. "Do you love me?" she says
and says, until the dog, sensing perhaps

its own awful speechlessness, tries to bolt,
but she holds it by the collar and will not
let go, until, having come closer,
I hear the rest of it. I hear it all.

. . .

She's got the dog's furry jowls in her hands,
she's speaking precisely
into its laid-back, quivering ears:
"Say it," she hisses, "say it to me."

MYOPIA

My half-blind lover mourned last night:
by the skylight enclosed, a thousand stars were only "dust
or back-lit fog," she said. She was sad,
until kiss by kiss her kisses climbed from chest
to neck to chin then cheek, and stopped.
I opened my eyes, and that's when she saw them.

"Don't move," she said. "Don't blink."
There were other worlds in my eyes,
pried open so wide at last I could not see,
as each constellation did not fall
but wobbled and slid, until a tear rolled loose
and dried in her lip-close breath.

And this morning, as she stepped from the shower
and wound her hair in a towel, she saw in the mirror,
or thought she saw, some new freckle, some unlikely blemish,
and still dripping leaned in, her shoulders bejeweled,
in the window's glow silver droplets trailing down
the dome in the small of her back.

So close then, she leaned so near the mirror
a sleepy moth of breath went winging there
and her breasts kissed her breasts against the glass.
Farsighted, I had to take a step away to see, then another.
I could see stars falling, and that clearly lucky man,
so close to her, as he parted and parted his hair.

DISCRETION

Wearing only moonglow
    and the fire's final shawls of smoke,
she made her way from the tent
    at 2 a.m., then squatted to pee,

and the heavenly light showed me everything:
    its cool tongues of silver lapping mountain
stones and the never-motionless leaves
    of aspens, licking her back, her hips,

haunches, and more, illuminating even the deep
    green eyes of whatever animal it was
that watched her from the forest then —
    a deer, I believed, and still believe,

though I confess I did not rise that night
    to make sure, did not shine my light or murmur
but waited, letting my head
    as she returned settle slowly back

down to the pillow made of my clothes
    and welcomed her shivering
back into the tent, from which
    I had sworn I would not look.

POOR ANIMALS

But the animals have no money, she says.
They're poor. So I say no and explain
the light and the dark, how one is endlessly
spent on food, the other rest,
like hamburgers and hotels, I say.

But they have no houses, no walls
or rooms, she says, no beds to rest on.
And so I take her hand and walk her
into the woods, where she lies
in their trampled sleep spots and samples

a rosehip, then a fist of autumn grasses.
She spits them out, and points
through the undergrowth to where
they watch us, two does and two
yearling fawns, hiding here, where the houses are.

I would tell her anything. She asks
about the fathers then, as gunfire
from beyond the far ridge tumbles by, a sound
as sourceless to her as the wind.
It's warm. A last hatch of flies zings alive,

and then she answers her own question.
They are at work, she says, teaching and singing
and selling, and the bears are the police,
and the birds are the drivers, and the air
is the hospital of the flies.

LATER THAT DAY

Because I did not want to walk far from home,
I stopped in a clearing and looked back:
the house's west gable, those two ancient pines

out front. All thorns and hooks the mountainside
I walked. Late summer and no rain
for weeks—ten weeks ago

exactly, another Tuesday,
third of July; see, I'd marked it
on the calendar. So dry even the air

as I breathed it crumbled to dust,
and the dogs, matted with blown seed pods,
shook and scratched and seemed forlorn.

And then looking down I saw
that all the clearing before me
was pocked, divoted, dished, depressions

dappled in its grass by bedding deer.
First the old dog lay down in one, and then the pup
turned around twice and flopped in another.

What was I to deny the sadness,
the bone-weary resignation, of dogs?
So I lay myself down in a third cote of grass,

curled fetal and took in the old fallen sleep smells
some buck or doe had given up
only the night before—

. . .

and it was sweet with unknowing, all
stillness and starlight among the slashes of thorns,
where we lay and slept like prey.

WASHING MY FACE

Dawn at the kitchen sink, sunrise still
an hour off, and out the window
the birch tree's swirling: a wind through the courtyard's
done it, stirred the loosening leaves
among dozens of goldfinches frantic
in its branches, feeding on the fat catkins,
and even in this soft, constant mist of rain
the tiny petals, nearly iridescent, glitter
as they fall, a snow of shed skins anointing
the phalanxes of blown irises and the black cat, Lily,
who rises through it all
to take the most careless finch,
just as the rest of the flock, as one — a wedge
of child-sized feathery fists — blinks
from the limbs and vanishes
down the canyon wall
even before Lily hits the ground, before
the column of water fallen from the faucet
enters the open, dry basin of my hands.

FISH DREAMS

She thinks the caught trout's eye must see
a monstrous face, for after all
its slick belly boils in her acid hand
and the hook's fluke knits the delicate jaw
half-closed. But I am not so sure.

Could you, so landed, understand
the majesty of God might live
among ten thousand types of fire?
Such beautiful meats we also might have been,
happily bereft of love and the black pearl

of emptiness our solitude protects.
Except she puts the hook and line aside
and enters the river and kneels there,
asking the current to kiss the flesh her now
flameless hands would caress again to life.

Narrow and cold the fish's world, and sleepless too,
they say. But think of the long night winter must be,
how, nuzzling the dark silt depths,
even a trout might dream of her—that hand,
the bottomless sky, the same terrible blue of her eye.

AFFIRMATIONS

I am in favor of this pair of ruffed grouse
who in the midst of the snow storm feasted long
and obliviously on the wizened, bittersweet,
long-fermented berries of the mountain ash.
I am also in favor of the old dog,
who did not mean to frighten the deer,
and while I regretted that I could no longer watch
as snow accumulated along the doe's back,
I am still in favor of the path it ran to get away,
although its running is what frightened the grouse.
And while it is too bad that in their wobbling,
soaring glide, both grouse struck the window
I stood in front of and were instantly killed,
let there be no doubt that I am in favor
of the tenderness of each bird's breast skin
and the ease with which it tears and folds away
with its feathers to expose the pink, warm meat of the breast.
For I am in favor of this odd infinitive verb,
to breast, as I breast one by one the supple front
meats from each grouse,
these limp-necked birds whose meat
I am most deeply in favor of, quick-fried in butter,
with a skiff of salt and a rasher of coarsely ground pepper
poured on, all of which, of course, I am in favor of as well,
as I am in favor of the butter's hot graceful glide
across the skillet and the propane's dank waft up
through copper pipe to the burner of the stove
and the blue flame tipped with yellow
that blossomed at the touch of my match.
I am also in favor of the wine, and of the grapes
that bless us so many miles from their vines,
just as I am in favor of how the sun going down now

casts its light precisely through the gap
beneath the far cloud's edge — the end of this very storm —
and the lip of the turning earth,
and makes as it does an immediate billion icy rainbows in the air,
an explosion so blinding that for a second
I am staggered and take hold
of the kitchen counter, just as the house lets go its stays
and glides toward the night,
as though it too believed as I do
that at the end there would be another day
just like this one.

IN AN ABANDONED ORCHARD

Name them apples, these shoe-stiff sags,
dangling, freckled by doors, the open ports
of pomace-drunk fruit wasps six weeks ago dead.

Furtive at first, the doe arrives, examining shadows,
nosing the lumpen ground for infirm
fly blown halves, ecstatically mouthing.

She leaps and rises, lightly, so lightly
it cannot be believed she does not fly
but turns and turns beneath a bland, inconsequential sky.

The last fruit dangles and she hangs by desire beneath it,
in the crosshairs turning — her slender knees,
from the ground where she walks in a broth of muddy hearts.

THATCHER BITCHBOY

She had brought home just a single white wing was all,
only that one through all the hellish August weeks
the fat man's chickens kept disappearing into,
and that one wing I buried myself in the manure pile
behind the barn, so that by the time he finally arrived,
Fat Man oozing from his high-backed truck
like a gristly hock onto the hot black skillet of the county road,
mostly all I felt was the least yawny pang of nerves.
I sat with my dog by the front porch.
"Thatcher bitchboy?" he asked,
and I allowed as how she was.
"Daddyhome?" he croaked,
and soon we all were there,
Daddy and me, that good bitch hound of mine sleeping
in a mottle of the day's last sun and shade, and the fat man
brandishing his blurred implicational snapshots.
There rose then a cloud of Daddy's might-could-bees
and a cloud also of Fat Man showly-izzes,
the sudden stormification of
which could have been why the sky itself
came on so holy and dark just then, a dreadnought cloak
I hoped the Goddumb damn dog would run off under,
but it was only when the light from Momma's
lamp in the living room window showed them there,
that it ended, and the fat man tied a rope
to the collar that convicted her,
and she licked his blunt and bulbous fingers with love
and servility ("tastez lack chickin doe-nit daug," he chortled to the dirt).
Good cur hound, your eyes on me leaving were a blue
I believed the starved-blood likes of God's own ledger,
all the betrayals in all the lands of earth and more
recorded therein, a blue like the lost unredeemable sky

I would myself be forever falling into,
some heaven of hellfires and ice
I have since that mouthhot night learned to breathe in
as though it were the exhalations of the finest funereal orchids,
an air I believed would teach me at last
how to pray, and most certainly
God help me
what for.

MUMMY OF A MOUSE

Spit back to sun by an owl or a snake,
here's this frail leather purse, gutless
and seemingly de-boned, but stiff enough to be held
upright by the pink slip of its tail
until, peering into the gut's open gash, I see
the sky come through as two points bilateral
to the snout, the mouse-eye view

of a blinding cosmos. The question is,
as it always is, what now? Should I
save it, this sarcophagus of minimal skin,
this hide bauble mouse mummy, this
memento of vacancy and death?
I've got enough saved bones at home to build
a mythical beast, some bird wolf

or the spawn of a bison and a hawk.
Near the front door, the skull of a gray whale
must always house a mouse or two,
and perhaps this sad sack himself tarried there
once, in the manner of the hunted, praying
in the manner of every fearful thing,
cowering inside the great gray brain chamber

of a beast a hundred thousand times
his size, like the last breath bubble
or a dream of dying, like the soul
misunderstood and misconstrued,
like a man in the hand of God,
so tiny and powerless that, though it will do
no good, God whispers to him, *Go! Run! Run!*

QUIET NIGHT

The bat's opened thorax blips
    —that's its heart
beating, says the boy—and its mouth bites
    at the air, and the cat
that brought it down sits two steps below
    and preens, while the pale cone
shed by the porch light makes and remakes itself
    with the shadows of miller, moth, and midge.
Listen, the darkness just under the stars
    is threaded with passings:
nighthawks and goatsuckers, the sleepy respirations of the forest,
    and the owl that asks first for a name,
then it leaves its spar
    and spreads a silence
so vast and immobile
    you can hear whole migrations inside it,
the swoons, the plummets, the bland ascensions
    of souls.

BRIDGE

Red Wolf Crossing, Snake River

You must understand the river
was a river then
not a pool behind a dam
above a pool behind a dam
above a pool behind a dam
and so on
I could go on
but see how the flow of the poem here is likewise unaesthetically halted
though this was then I'm talking about
and there was no poetry then
no poetry at all
that was not spoken and spoken
chanted and sung
as the river itself might be said to have sung and sung
though that would be to personify to sentimentalize
to make of the river a conscious being aware
of its own voice
aware of the other-way rush of the salmon
which this myth would have as the first bridge

young Red Wolf and the woman he loved
and chased among the drying racks and alder fires
the woman who laughed
and sprinting left him flat-footed and breathless
on the shore
her feet so lightly coming down
on the broad silver backs and rolling blue bellies
on the rounded red sides of the sockeyes
that she was in his eyes walking
on water though nothing
made a god of her any more than she herself
on the far shore

when she shed her robe and smiled and made ready
from which also comes the word redd
river womb for egg and milt
and Red Wolf or the father of Red Wolf
or the fathers of all men
leaped and began

and thus it is now
when the river is a pool behind a dam
above a pool behind a dam
and so on
that the surface of the bridge in the elegiac last light
sometimes takes on the colors of their original skins
and not even the most sadly prudish of men and women
can fail to see the huge erotic symbolism
of the bridge
which is after all only concrete and steel
an elegant and unintentional cenotaph
built so someone must have thought to further
the mercantile and industrial needs of nowhere in particular
where nothing much has happened
but ten thousand years of miracles
before the beginning of the beginning of the end
of time

ANECDOTAL FENCEPOST

Dead center in a hanging meadow,
halfway up a side canyon slope,
there's this orphan post raised by wolves,
this thing of one world implanted
in the other, without history or blood,
neither the lineage of tetanus nor the heraldry of rust.

There's enough barbed wire in this state
to string a line to the moon and back.
From a plane it's a Frankenstein stitchery,
a backroom facelift, but there's no wire I can see,
and quarter-round cedar fenceposts
do no occur spontaneously in nature.

This one, by the fine approximate plumb
of it, looks as though it were dropped
from a great height by the mother of all
nesting eagles, or one of those new western ranchers,
the ones who eschew the blue healer for the fax
and beeper, the quarter horse for the helicopter.

And though I wander around it, my widening gyre,
my careful forensic finds no line, no
other post anywhere, only this, which,
because it is wood, will fall,
the slovenly wilderness at last
avenging its mystery, its jarring illogic —
. . .

but not before a meadowlark,
at least thirty times in an hour,
alights on top and recites, in many notes,
its song, which sounds to me like reason.

CLEMENCY

Over the trough, the long face of the horse,
and croaking dead center in a hoof print,
a toad—all the while the redwing blackbirds
drilling their whistly bells. February,
and a sudden, unearthly spring. God above me,
I am halfway through this field, a feeding,
the season, my life. If it pleases you, then hear me:
what I would ask is ten thousand more afternoons
like this, though doubtless the unkilled fleas, scintillant
and fat, will bedevil the dogs and cats,
and a few, skin-weary, will fall among
the rumpled bedclothes to catch us there,
my lover and me, and marry us done.
But please, just let this long light be garlanded by birds
and the garrulous, sloe-eyed toad.
Let the mare scratch her ear all down the length of me.
Let her breathe where the lick of memory wants.

LIVES OF THE ANIMALS

One neighbor's got a heeler
named Job; another's got just
a snapshot or two, a frou-frou,
nappy poodle, yapping
and vanished without a trace.

Cats, if they survive
to adulthood, fare better,
though there was an honest shortage
of kittens one summer,
thanks to the hordes of owls and hawks.

Then there are the weeds,
the stick-tights and teasels,
brain-festering cheatgrass depth charges
down the ears, the eye-slashing
barely visible star thistle spines.

There are bored boys
with BB and pellet guns and drivers
on the country roads
with nowhere to swerve to.
There's terrible heat and terrible cold.

For the rest of us—the biped,
broad-nailed, featherless master race—
there's only black ice and bad driving,
deep fats and a government's erector set
experiments with nuclear bombs.

• • •

Then there's the annual spring plague
of ticks, and the nightly sessions
on the living room floor,
grooming like chimps. First,
the dogs, then the cats,

then the kids, then last of all,
later, the two of us, the tender skin
at the base of the scalp,
the tenderer skin of the crotch,
and once, my lover

plucked from the tip of my ear,
with a divot of skin,
a tick already fastened on
and fattening with my blood.
She kissed the wound there

and did not stop
kissing, but held the tick
between her thumb and forefinger
all through the love that followed,
then expelled what I'd left her

in the toilet, wrapped the tick
in a wad of tissue,
dropped it there too,
and came to bed.
All that night I was moving

. . .

in my sleep, running the dank
weedy channels after pheasants
or stalking the shrews and voles
and meadow mice that abound here.
All that night the scent of skin

was on me, the scent of bodies
opened toward the blood.
By morning I'd have sworn
it was all a dream. I was
the only human animal awake

at that hour. In a wedge of sun
the cats lay tangled
and rumbling. The dog's tail thumped,
a tentative knock as I rose.
But there was the red speck

on my pillow, and in the pale light
of the bathroom, a black mole
afloat in a sea of dross
and sodden tissue. I held my finger
down to the surface, and the tick scrambled on.

Now the dog's up and yawning,
the cats yammer for their food.
True to form, there's Job
outside, his hide a matted mass
of burrs and thorns,

• • •

behind his ear a cluster
of ticks swollen fat as grapes.
I call him to the door. He's meek
and grateful for attention.
I scratch his chin

and nestle that rescued tick
deep in the fur around his neck.
I make coffee. I slice a peach
and take my breakfast on the porch,
where the cats rub figure-eights

around my ankles, where the dogs
await a nibble of toast. The sun is warm
and the breeze is cool. This is the world,
my brothers, we enter yet again,
our arms flung open wide.

AFTER THE COYOTES' SONG

Now night is clearly darker than before
and smells more still, its star wick trimmed
audibly down. Now all rodents are emboldened,
all owls through their talons knowing,
down the limb-bones and capillary fretwork
of roots and holes, that every living thing's
about to bolt,
                 even the tiny dumb animal
of my sleep, having for how many hours now
cowered under the rock of possible dreams—
look, there it goes, a whip of tail
running for its life, and the owl soars up
as silent on its nightmare wings as sleep's breath is
to the sleeper.

HORSEFLIES

After the horse went down
    the heat came up,
and later that week
    the smell of its fester yawed,
an open mouth of had-been air
    our local world was licked
inside of, and I,

the boy who'd volunteered at twilight —
    shunts of chawed cardboard
wadded up my nostrils
    and a dampened bandanna
over my nose and mouth —
    I strode then

into the ever-purpler sink
    of rankness and smut,
a sloshful five-gallon bucket of kerosene
    in my right hand,
a smoking railroad fusee
    in my left,
and it came over me like water then,

into my head-gaps and gum
    rinds, into the tear ducts
and taste buds and even
    into the last dark tendrils
of my howling, agonized hair
    that through the windless half-light
hoped to fly from my very head,

• • •

and would have, I have no doubt, had not
      the first splash of kerosene
launched a seething skin
      of flies into the air
and onto me, the cloud of them
      so dense and dark my mother in the distance
saw smoke and believed as she had feared

I would, that I had set my own
      fool and staggering self aflame,
and therefore she fainted and did not see
      how the fire kicked
the other billion flies airborne
      exactly in the shape
of the horse itself,

which rose for a brief quivering
      instant under me, and which for a pulse thump
at least, I rode — in a livery of iridescence,
    · in a mail of exoskeletal facets,
wielding a lance of swimming lace —
      just as night rode the light, and the bones,
and a sweet, cleansing smoke to ground.

FOLLOWING SNAKES

Esses, esses, a glassine imaginary axis
rigid from the utterly linear and straightforward head:
I follow the elegant and anachronistic rattlesnake carefully,
for he would rather not leave the warm path
willingly but, spring and all and him half-blind
from molting, happily would he coil and fight
whatever thumping thing comes blundering behind him.

I could wait him out, but I have my stick after all
and a few body lengths between us, and also a plenitude
of stones nearby. I have killed and skinned his kind
before, but mostly I love the way he moves
out front of me, an undulant ornament on the car of my going
toward the river, except now I see the other one
headed our way, or his way, a snake so identical

in cross-hatch scale and motion, I cannot believe
I myself do not walk out of a mirror and into this other scene.
Now they are chin to chin and rise and twine
like paper streamers, a bunting of meat and bone,
then a ball of bulges or a fist two long fingers thick.
Their rattles tick and chatter, they are belly to belly
when the dog trots past and over them

unawares and keeps on going, bound for the river.
That's when they coil then spin
and slant off the trail to the brush. Cheatgrass signals
their going, a thin green wedge nodding off
from where they met, and from me, who mourns
a little, who loves all undulant things and things that mate,
though now they may wait near the path I walk.

SNAKE IN THE TROUGH

It must have rested a moment or two
    on the trough's west edge,
that rattlesnake, it must have climbed
    slow as a stem
up the ancient cedar plank side,
    over nodules of tar
heat-softened and oozed from a seam,
    to bask on the neck-rounded
splintering rim and test
    the fierce August air with its tongue.
It might have turned then, curled,
    hunched sidelong at its middle,
and leaned at least half its length
    down toward the water.
In a dry season, in a drought
    most of a decade long,
the old spring, the one the locals called
    "Everlasting," had slowed
to a warble of semi-constant drops,
    and in the heat of the day
the lone horse in the pasture
    could drink it dry at one long lap.
But this was morning, and maybe
    the horse still hung its head then
under the only tree's shade,
    and the snake would have
gone down then like an expensive machine,
    a well-oiled, hydraulic arm
toward the low water, so low
    if you had been there
you would have had to move too close
    to see it dip its slick scaled chin

into the sky-shimmering surface,
    where your own face would have floated too,
as the horse's must have soon.

A snake would not have needed much
    water—a drop, maybe three or four—
but then, its drinking mechanism
    inefficient, maybe,
or maybe just basking in the tepid
    watery languor there,
it stayed and stayed,
    its head immobile, dreaming,
and its tense anchoring end relaxed and unclenched,
    which caused its fall
—no ooze or elegant peristalsis now,
    no slitherward unweighting
and lungestrike
    but a wet thud and thrash,
and then its rapid esses
    swimming.
The wedge of its head rising
    at each attempt out would have been
no more than the span of a man's hand
    up the moss-slick sides toward the top—
all of which the landowner
    surmised long after, after he heard the boom,
the kick of the Morgan gelding's
    heavily shod front hoof
against the trough, and after he saw
    the old horse rear back,
water coursing from its muzzle
    and a yard-long snake dangling

from its upper lip like the strap of a broken headstall.

    Though the man did not take time

to grab a snake-killing shovel or hoe,

    still there was the wire gate to pass through,

the johnson-bar on a chain

    unslinging the tightly strung closure,

but slowly, so that he only caught

    on a lucky glance up the snake

at a seventh or eighth head whip

    flung loose into bunchgrass

and wild timothy,

    and the gelding at a dead panicked run

taking loose the fence's

    two top strands—the popped staples

dropping down the pasture's line

    like a squall of audible rain—

and tumbling over headfirst,

    its neck-broke last thrashes subsiding

just as the man arrived.

    That was what he saw then, that,

and the punctures of the fangs

    on the horse's lip, and he wondered:

the wounds from the barbed wire

    not so much different

really than a snake's, so he scuffed the dirt

    where he stood then fastened

a chain around the dead gelding's hocks

    and hooked the other end

to the tractor's bucket,

    so that the carcass might be dragged out

and hoisted into the renderer's truck.

    This was a thousand pound useful animal after all,

even dead, and the dust
    it would neither be nor raise again
mattered less than the knowing,
    and the knowing did not matter much at all,
the snake in the trough
    being everything by now, the myth
of it a parable he could keep
    on living by, as he walked the fields
and pastures and killed
    as he came across it
every snake he encountered there,
    believing each time he did
that this was surely the one,
    the snake he feared, its curse
and thirst having felled a horse.

SWALLOWS

Gnatsnappers, say the old time canyon folk,
good bug gluttons, a pure summer blessing
upon us. And tonight, reliable as sunset
the swirl of just-hatched caddis flies
spins a shimmery halo over my head,
same spot every time, southeast edge
of the eaves, just above the hammock's
elliptical sway. Swifts, too, they say,
squeaking acrobats in their feeding flights.

The cliff below the house is festooned
with their nests, tumors of dried mud
dun in the daily sun. Once
I climbed the cottonwood there,
to carve my lover's name and mine
above a sky-high fork, and was halfway
through the curved, enclosing heart
when I heard their rattle behind me.

What's a fool for love in a tree but a fiend,
each ounce of unfledged nestlings
no more than a long arm's length away?
As I worked loose the kerf of bark,
completing my heart, they came closer,
the racket of chitters and purls
a back-of-the-neck whisk of feathers.

That night on the porch they would not come near,
the caddis hatch smorgasbord above me
gone begging, and I, in the hammock's
sleepy respirations, knew exactly why.
Puny, limb-borne Icarus, I had strayed too high

in the neighborhood of open air, what wings
I could fashion, just a man's crooked heart
and a metaphor beginning with names.

Live and learn, I say. Tonight those thumb small
nestlings clamoring for bugs are adults
come home to nest themselves, and we are pupils
my lover and I, in the long white eye
of the hammock looking up.
As fast as the light itself, swallows enter
the satin flutter of the flies,
take one or two and set the whole swirl
widely spinning, before it eases back again.

The hammock sways.
Our children play alongside us,
oblivious, or used to miraculous flights,
though something's in the light as it falls.
It calls them on, bugs and birds,
a boy and girl at play, the lovers
who made them another nest of limbs.

If I rose now and stood astride her
in the uneasy dusk, a pale human version
of airborne in the hammock's motion
and lift, I could ease my love-struck head
into the caddis fly cloud and feel
the passage of the swallows' wings.
And I could see, perhaps, in the last light
shining on the cottonwood's high fork,

• • •

that carved heart saying out our names
among the leaves, where no one goes
but swallows and wrens, where it is touched
by wind and rain and nothing else.
But I stay where I am, until the flies alight
and the birds give way to bats, until the stars
come on, showing me one more time
all I know of the sky.

HIGHWAY 12, JUST EAST OF PARADISE, IDAHO

The doe, at a dead run, was dead
the instant the truck hit her.
In the headlights I saw her tongue
extend and her eyes go shocked and vacant.
Launched at a sudden right angle — say
from twenty miles per hour south to fifty
miles per hour east — she skated
many yards on the slightest toe-edge tips
of her dainty deer hooves, then fell
slowly, inside the speed of her new trajectory,
not pole-axed but stunned, away
from me and the truck's decelerating pitch.
She skidded along the right lane's
fog line true as a cue ball,
until her neck caught a sign post
that spun her across both lanes and out of sight
beyond the edge. For which, I admit, I was grateful,
the road there being dark, narrow, and shoulderless,
and home, with its lights, not far away.

PROGRESS

Web by web the ruined work of spiders
    marked his progress up the trail.
Some made clear by the right haft of light
    he waved away with his stick,
others clinging full across the face
    or making of his dark shirt
and jeans an odd diaphanous
    tweed not found in any store.
He never once broke stride or slowed,

though coming back he saw,
    by the tatters of the webs,
wind-swung, tangled and combined,
    two red-brown, heavy-bottomed spiders,
each devouring the other. Mandible to abdomen,
    they gnawed, and a pair of pale egg swags
swung under them, pendulous, albuminate,
    by gravity drawn down,
each one adorned by a single shimmering blue fly.

WINTER BALE

Not a scent so much as a bouquet
of smells, that stable: old wood, horse flesh,
the round sweet buds of manure;
molasses, oats, leather, hay.

In the ancient bushel basket a nest
of twine, now the red taut plunk of it cut
from the bale, as puffed up
out of the flakes comes dust

from the fields a year before,
and a stiff, sleepy bull snake oozes
over the cold floor and into the stall
where the edgy stallion waits for hay.

CAFFEINE

Awaken! Now tankards, river-tipplers, scandalous vats
vast with bitternuts and light: we will keen and whine,
a fine implosive fury of whodom and me.
Come, gadflies, be your congressman's crosses
to bear, your bones be sirens to the nails. All hail,
by the way, and even snow and sleet,
are only the heavenly incumbencies of rain.
I do not love the world any more
or less than you do. Now and then
I need a lift, now and then a hammer,
a blade, a frayed rope, or a bullet.
Everyone's weary of the God groans on TV
and the glowing-after magazine angels of Armani.
I'm a middle class American, by crackee,
I know my lefts from my trickled down leftovers,
these slender portfolios my brothers
and my mother claim to read. And I'm not bitter.
I'm blessed and sped up, buzzed and incorruptible.
There is no royalty in poetry and Emily is its mother.
See here? Between the lines the skulk of pulp,
the vaporous ghosts of trees, the spice that Marco Polo left with.
Deer lick, the flick of the wrist, the mark
that follows amen. Here comes the cat,
who loves me in her way, and who eases the wedge
of her head in my cup and laps every morning
the powdery black dregs and begs for more.
She is deadly, she endures my love. She's killed
yet another songbird and has, the preachers insist,
of heaven, no hope at all,
and no reason but the flesh to go on.

AGENCY

They stumble now and then, the deer,
like any other walking thing, even those
not unlike themselves, four-legged
but less elegant and fleet — cows in a bog,
the clumsy, over-bred, domesticated dogs —
though most of the deer I've seen go down
have suffered in some way the agency of man:
a buck at full run dropped
by a lucky shot, its sleek forequarters
folded back and the early autumn dust
blowing up around it in a cloud.
The genderless whitetail haunch and flag
flashing through headlights and crashing
on the sinew tight wires of a three-strand fence.
And then this morning, the last,
the smallest one of a band of seven does —
not stepping like the others but playful —
leaping from the berm that separates the woods
from the often-plowed, sheet ice driveway.
I was watching from the dining room window when she fell
and I spilled a little coffee, flinching.
Then a few of the others looked up and saw me there,
their amazing, ludicrous tails spontaneously rising.
And everything stopped, even the pale scrim
of the driest cold snow ceased coming down
as we waited.
          And when the fallen one rose
she rose on just three legs, the fourth not
tucked up but dangling, a slender dead weight.
I was crouched at the long glass. I thought I might
dabble at the coffee stain,
but I was frozen, motionless, hardly breathing,

until one of those outrageous, many-snowflake flotillas
came down, tumbling, ungainly,
to disappear into the white, into what had come before,
into the mountain's long seasonal slope,
and then they were moving again, up, back
over the snaggled, plow-strewn berm and into the woods,
where a few dry grasses might still be
turned up here and there, where already fallen snow scraped
the bellies even of the moose who walked there,
the 9th of February, 2001, winter
almost halfway gone.

KISSING A HORSE

Of the two spoiled, barn-sour geldings
we owned that year, it was Red—
skittish and prone to explode
even at fourteen years—who'd let me
hold to my face his own: the massive labyrinthine
caverns of the nostrils, the broad plain
up the head to the eyes. He'd let me stroke
his coarse chin whiskers and take
his soft meaty underlip
in my hands, press my man's carnivorous
kiss to his grass-nipping upper half of one, just
so that I could smell
the long way his breath had come from the rain
and the sun, the lungs and the heart,
from a world that meant no harm.

"DOG"

For how many days had she shaken?
She'd shaken and shaken, standing there
hunched, unable to walk or lie,

until exhaustion overtook her
and pivoting on one leg she folded down—
shaking, always shaking—and did not sleep,

not even on the last night or the next morning,
when he gathered her into his arms like a sack.
She wheezed then, as though

the weight of her so borne
were a kick to the ribs,
and she drooled onto his sleeve

then lay in the grass
where he placed her looking up,
her half-hairless tail a faint pulse of approval.

And he raised the rifle,
placed the bead in the notch
of the sight, first

on the slope of her slant forehead,
and then among the mottled cowlicks
of the coat across her chest—

and she died,
                was gone *like that,*
the bullet still chambered in its shell,
his finger barely nestled to the smooth curl

. . .

of the rifle's trigger of brass.
For he was so intent on this awful chore
he might not have noticed her dead at all,

if the shaking—for how many days
had it been?—if the shaking had not come to seem
the very motion taken in her by life itself,

the shaking, the shaking, a being that blood by blood
thumps through his own brotherly bones,
as rain or sap moves

through the billion suckling root mouths
his digging has exposed
and to which he feeds her,

saying over her grave the single word
she had always known herself by,
never understanding it was no name at all.

NORTHERN LIGHTS

Nestled in his hands, the slack, leaden anus
    still attached, it shines inhuman, iridescent,
unlike the spilled viscera —
    the intestines' pearly diminishing ropes,
a fading sheen of bile leaked from the liver,
    the lungs and heart, a sleek degreening pancreas —
all going dull, scrimmed in the kill light of cold, actual air.
    It throbs without motion. Nacreous muscle,
gleaming, as though the bullet when it killed her lungs
    had left her heart still alive,
and the last blue, breathless pulse thumps
    came to rest where a sap lure
of oestrus and rut had been boiling.
    He's got to slit her hocks and hoist her
from a fir tree's limb. He's got to peel and pull
    the hide and hack away her head, section her
mid-spine, and carry every quarter out,
    two miles south and a half mile down.
But he cannot get past this slab of gleaming flesh,
    its unmythical birth-lips and gate-gilding, muscular plush,
what it was, what it is now, in his mind's eye all the way
    to the truck, three times up and four times down,
when the day's light is gone and the beam
    of his headlamp has wilted just past his toes,
when the night forest ticks with the passage
    of shadows, and he emerges from the canopy of limbs
one last time into the frosted meadow before the road
    and sees in the northern sky

the arctic lights come tumbling and tossing,
    like a being in perfect motion, corporeal and vast,
sides and thighs and a luminous pulsating skin
    through which the brightest stars, in the ever colder night,
wetly shine, though all were fire once, and some are gone.

THE AFTERLIFE OF MOOSE
for Stephen Dunn

As the moose is obsessed, relentlessly
and with little or no variation, with food,
safety, and procreation, I am myself
obsessed of late with God, though by God
even I am uncertain What or Who I mean:
the word or the Word in the mouths
of those who use the word as a bludgeon;
the fabulous order of all disorderly things
or the perfect chaos that lives in straight lines;
all the succulent preliminary wines and kisses
or the thrust and plunge and plosive release.

I've been watching this particular bull
for a good while now, as he feeds
on the rich new shoots and shrub
by shrub moves slowly through the forest.
He knows I'm here. He eyes me
now and then. This morning I am in his mind
as God never is, and what I wish I knew
is whether or not I envy him that constant absence,
or whether doubt might not be
the source of all love,
all the shimmer of truth, the flavors of beauty.
Only a fool would see the moose's life
as easier or less than his own.
As for the afterlife, I'll take his chances.

THE CHURCH OF OMNIVOROUS LIGHT

On a long walk over the mountain you'd hear
them first, the pang and chorus
of their exultations, as though you'd strayed
out of Hawthorne into Cotton Mather—
such joyous remorse, such cranky raptures.

And you'd love their fundamental squawking,
little Pentacostal magpies, diminutive
raven priests. You'd walk into their circle
like a drag queen into a Texas truckstop—
silence first, then the caterwauls, the righteous gacks.

Someone's gutted out a deer is all.
In the late autumn snow you'd see the deacons'
tracks—ursine, feline, canine—sweet eucharist of luck
and opportunity for them all. Take and eat,
clank the birds, but not too much. It might be a while.

You'd wonder, yes you would,
and maybe nudge with the toe of your boot
the seeming rigidity of the severed esophagus,
gently belled, like a deaf man's antique horn,
and the breathless lungs subsiding to carnate blood.

You'd want to go, but you'd want to stay;
you'd want a way to say your part in the service
going on: through high windows
the nothing light, the fourteen stations
of the clouds, the offertory of snow.

. . .

Imagine the brethren returned, comical,
hopping in surplice and cassock, muttering,
made dyspeptic by your presence there, but hopeful too,
that something might yet come and open
your coarse, inexplicable soul to their sight.

IN TIME

The great pine fallen by the wind
lay across the game trail down
from the ridge to the creek
and has in all the years since been

leaped, scratched, and scrambled over—
tenderized, hoof-chiseled—
until today, when down all its half-limbed
unbroken length there is only this

one gap to pass through,
and I do, for the hundredth time
I've walked here, going always back
through deeper seasons of drought and fire,

seasons of plenty and seasons of want,
to the pummeled heart of its long death
and longer life, to when it first rose up into the sun
which had just the day before shown Keats his pale shadow.

SWEETBREADS

"What foods these morsels be!"
—The Joy of Cooking

Thymus of the neck, and of the stomach,
pancreas: it sounds like a pair
of demi-gods in Greek, don't you think?
Through lean times my mother specialized
in "organ foods": the rubbery beef heart,
simmered several hours under pressure,
no less rubbery but having stewed by then
a good dark pint of flavorful blood broth;
pork brains breaded and fried
but in any cooked guise always and only gray;
the various livers—calf's on good days,
steer's on bad; kidneys, tongue, and even these
soaked, blanched, and quick-fried odd delicacies
once or twice: the butcher was sweet on her,
you see.

        Therefore, in my mother's honor,
I sauté not just the tender liver
of this small but fine bull elk—
quarter inch slices slathered in onions—
but the sweetbreads too, pancreas (which means
"all meat" anyway) and thymus (which means
nothing but what it says), and in addition,
in honor of my father, who hated
every visceral tidbit she served him
but loved my mother beyond all sweet reason,
I toss in the unlucky bull's fresh balls
dredged in flour and brown them both up golden,
crisp and hot on the outside, warm and pink
cut in two. They bobble on the platter,
among the slabs of liver and wrinkled sweets,
like four domes fallen in a ruins of flesh

and fire—sweetbreads my elders understood:
all those dead dears who wouldn't waste a thing,
who at the scent of cooking meat closed in
and breathed it, who murmured as they chewed,
who kissed the salts from each other's lips,
then went to bed those nights thankful
and sated and blessed with a hunger
that would lead in time to me.

MERCY

We grabbed the huge, ancient trough
by its chin-rounded oaken rim,
dragged it aside, and there they were:

in a cup of horsehair and hay
a fistful throng of newborn mice,
squirming in the sudden light—

pink pods, like the seeds of someday fingers.
The engine of the tractor
thrummed, and a new trough dangled

by chains from its bucket, a chime
of galvanized steel ringing
in the cold spring rain.

Everywhere on the farm, the signs of mice,
their dark curds and commas, parenthetical
with disease. Boy at a summer job,

I stepped up then and sent the nest on a soccer kick—
horsehair, hay, pellets of pale flesh—
sailing through the heavy iron bars of the gate

to the noxious wallow of the hogs, which
as it happened, was empty then,
the day before having been their last.

HELPFUL

—for my parents

1.

She did not know he was on the ladder
at all, until by some unlikely coincidence
of lucky perambulation and peripheral light,
she glimpsed the vaguest, leggy shadow of the thing
tumble past the living room window as she walked by.

It was cold outside and he was badly broken.
These facts, in the order a strong wind
resolves a flung deck of cards to, she relates
to me on the phone. I have never heard my mother
so undone by life, or not by life

but by my father, seventy-seven and absent
as he spoke from his hospital bed, spitted
and turning over some fire that is time
and place, neither here nor there, now or then,
in the jarred, delicate peach of his mind.

And of course, by the time I arrived, many flights
and a rental car later, the winter storm
he'd meant to beat had beaten everything down,
and still the gutters were clotted with sweetgum balls.
This is what you do, I thought, driving,

the snow likewise driving, the white familiar
awful other-wayness of it making a way back
bathysphere of the rented Ford. I was diving
into the past where I never was a man,
I was seeing in the slashed and staticky air

. . .

this broken elder soul who had become my father,
I was imagining who I would have to be
in the event of events as likely as snow or rain.

2.

Except that now, two years hence, my father's hip
in the storm cloud sky of the X ray
looks like the scale model steering gear

of a vintage Buick, and that's all right. He walks
and chills to the bone from the hip bone out.
And if he still cannot say how it was
he fell, he remembers that, later on, I was there,
helping my mother, which is what matters most.

I have told him more: of haranguing the careless
neurologist, pressing the impatient, soon-to-be
vacationing GP for early release, the walker
of stark aluminum, the toilet contrivance
that cut the distance between standing and sitting.

But still today he is most impressed that I shoveled
the driveway clear: a foot of rained-on
crusty snow, and under it the sheet of ice
that came as freezing rain, where I stopped,
just under the gutter, at the still-red,

. . .

vivid, and terrifying puddle of his blood,
frozen on the salt-pocked expanse of concrete.
I have not told him this: how it was pink at the edges,
but heart dark, liverish at the center; how there was a bolus of it,
thick as a thumb, I pried up and threw, like a stone, into the woods.

BEAR DREAMS

What had seemed to him in June just a few
five-petaled pink wild roses
was in fact a weeks long, slow-moving onslaught

of blossoms. He sees this now, of course,
in September, having come down from the house
to the edge of the deep undergrowth outside his fence,

fence that keeps his dogs inside, fence
the young bear had pushed against just minutes ago, paws resting
on the steel diamond links as it had looked

toward something the man couldn't see inside the yard.
At the very click of the back door's latch
the bear bolted away, looked back once

from the narrow gravel road, and was gone.
Beside the man the dogs pant and wait,
and there is nothing else in the world but the song

of a bird he wonders at but will not
seek out, neither in the branches of trees
nor the leaves and plates of the field guide,

preferring to portrait or flight the sourceless singing,
wanting less to unknow some words than their meanings.
The way "rose" suddenly means the bare skin of a girl

ten billion blossoms ago, who'd undressed and let him
look and only look and look at her looking back.
He'd wanted to see the whole soft machine of her, all the cogs

. . .

and stigmata. She wanted to see him seeing,
and that is what he remembers now, just the half-gone image
of his seeing, not what he saw, though now a twig dangles broken

from the bear's going away, and he sees how
a cool autumn wind sets the whole sprawling rose bush
nodding, and he knows the rose does not love

the bear or the birds or any man,
not even the early bees that bob inside and pollinate its flowers.
What a perfect five-petaled plucked roulette

a wild rose is: started right, she could never love me not.
And though he knows this opulence of hips, this abundance
of fruit and seed, could likely lure another, braver bear,

who'd take the fence and feast to its fill —
which in a bear is almost never — he also knows that
in the long winter's sleep that's coming, a bear too,

even the fullest, most sated of bears, will dream
and see as it could not in the midst of its feasting
all that is no longer there, those seeds of another hunger.

BREAKING TRAIL

So all night long the wind kept coming, gusts
and cloud strokes combing the beards
of the yellow pines, until this morning,
when every swatch of snow lay
whiskered as a dead man's cheek.

I hope that's true, the figure
of the corpse's beard, blithely growing.
I can hear my heart, you see,
the first long ski of the year, as though it
were the one breaking trail, not I.

Meanwhile the sky goes on glowering,
snow in its teeth, color of a bruise
set free of the skin. I love
the pure, unnerving solitude when I stop, silence
through which the animal of me gallops.

The light does not exist I see by
now, except for this one place
and the atmosphere of dreams. My lungs
ache, I do not think but remember
bless and bleed share the same derivation.

And now the snow I could smell
has married the wind, my face
feels sandblasted. Even when I stop
to listen, I hear nothing of my passage,
no heart thrump or lung rasp,

. . .

and then, on a long downslope,
gathering speed, I round a corner
and enter the motions of a herd of deer.
With me, away from me, they are
running, my heart among their hooves

synchronous and silent, the skis no more
than the sibilance of wind. I could touch
the flank of the doe alongside me,
a pattern of snow on her back
shows her heat—and then they're gone.

Six, eight, twenty—to the left and down:
they enter the shapes of the trees
as wind caresses the bellies of clouds.
And again I am deep inside my own life,
alone, led by hoof-sounds down.

ABOUT THE AUTHOR

Robert Wrigley's *Reign of Snakes* won the 2000 Kingsley Tufts Poetry Award. He teaches at the University of Idaho and lives with his wife, the writer Kim Barnes, and their children near Moscow, Idaho.